WRITERS

ON

WRITERS

Published in partnership with

**STATE LIBRARY
VICTORIA**
What's your story?

THE UNIVERSITY OF
MELBOURNE

WRITERS

JOSEPHINE ROWE

ON

BEVERLEY FARMER

WRITERS

Published by Black Inc.
in association with the University of Melbourne and State Library Victoria.

Black Inc., an imprint of Schwartz Books Pty Ltd
Level 1, 221 Drummond Street, Carlton VIC 3053, Australia
enquiries@blackincbooks.com
www.blackincbooks.com

State Library Victoria
328 Swanston Street, Melbourne Victoria 3000 Australia
www.slv.vic.gov.au

The University of Melbourne
Parkville Victoria 3010 Australia
www.unimelb.edu.au

9781760642310 (hardback)
9781743821572 (ebook)

A catalogue record for this
book is available from the
National Library of Australia

Cover design by Peter Long and Akiko Chan
Photograph of Josephine Rowe: Patrick Pittman
Photograph of Beverley Farmer: Christopher Deere
Text design by Peter Long
Typesetting by Akiko Chan

Printed in China by 1010 Printing.

THE HIGH SEASON

It is 1971 and she is thirty, working the high season in a taverna at the foot of Mount Olympus. She and her husband are often awake into the early hours, frying prawns, washing dishes. Then stealing a few hours' sleep in the car, until daybreak, when the fishermen haul their catches ashore and knock on the windscreen for coffee.

What she'll remember of these months: the wasps and wine and watermelon rinds, the octopuses pegged out spread-eagled to dry. Pausing in her work to lie moaning in the sand with morning sickness. The ocean periodically surging in to uproot their slender poplars. Running outside during storms to hold the saplings to the earth.

The season in that northern place was over after the Feast of the Virgin in mid-August. The sun had begun to have a chill in it; the sea filled with jellyfish – limpid medouses, *Medusas; and* tsouchtres *whose lash marked you like hot iron ... We stayed on the whole Autumn, watching the snow advance down Mount Olympus. Life was cold and unprofitable, but easy*, she writes, fifteen years later, at the edge of a different ocean, at the closing down of the Australian summer. March, and the holiday crowds have thinned, but the tide pools still hold the heat.

She will spend the next thirty years looking onto the sea from this small protrusion of shipwreck coast – *the beginning of the world, or the end of the world* – logging its moods, its changes, its flotsam and curious omens. The ancient *ever-presence* of the ocean, and the lights and warnings that sweep across it; the worlds teeming within, and the shifting geologies heaped at its threshold – *the leggy peninsulas, all coves, outcrops and arches, sandbanks, caverns, pitted cliffs strung with seaweed.*

All that washes up or crumbles away, or latches on tenaciously and thrives.

OTHER ROOMS

Attention to what is. Because whatever is added to the image hoard of one mind is an addition to the world. Not a permanent one, needless to say. What is permanent about a grain of fire in space? We believe in anything rather than accept that a whole world emblazoned inside the eggshell of the skull is fated for extinction.

Beverley Farmer, *The Bone House*

April in Rome. I was not yet lonely. Still considered myself inoculated against loneliness, having lived out of suitcases for several years, moving through a succession of cities where, for a while at least, no one knew me.

The idea of home was tucked into a few portable articles. A slender stack of books that had become talismanic through travel. Two palm-sized stones from Lake Huron. A painted wooden jewellery box that had belonged to my grandmother. A white gold ring, and another carved from red cedar. Letters from friends that had found me in Montreal, Toronto, Oakland, Hobart, New York. These had taken on a reassuring sense of continuity: *You are here*, regardless of the postmark. I carried them with me to Italy, though I knew it would only be six months.

In February, shortly after I arrived, it had snowed for the first time in six years, and children who had never seen snow before were let loose on it. Their parents plowed into it like children, demonstrating how to pack a ball from the powder-fine drift. I watched multigenerational snowball fights from eight floors above Viale di Trastevere, the terraces on the lower rooftops and surrounding balconies muted white. That final month of winter was over so quickly that is nearly all I remember of it, two years on: the one day of snow, and the day that followed – scuffing over frozen patches in the near-empty gardens of Villa Borghese towards gloaming, blue and gold air swirling with icy mica blown from the shoulders of headless statues.

All of March it poured torrents. But you could go into the Pantheon just to get out of the weather. The marvel of this was never lost on me – listening to the rain fall through the oculus, the reverent hush punctured at intervals by the booming prerecorded requests for silence in several languages.

The eighth-floor Trastevere studio was four rooms and a terrace so vast it would have fit the apartment again. The view afforded a lot of sky, the odd glimpse of ruins, the dismissed gasometer in Ostiense. A stone pine up in Villa Doria Pamphili that looked like a figure pissing into the wind. This view was mine, or what I might make of it, until the end of summer.

The apartment had been home to expat Australians Bertie and Lorri Whiting, a poet and a painter. After Bertie's death in 1989, Lorri gifted the studio to the Australia Council for the Arts as a residence for Australian poets, to honour her husband and his work. Somewhere in the piece, other writers – non-poets and lapsed poets – snuck in.

Forewords to B.R. Whiting's collections invoke wild parties at the studio, a raucous cohort of artists and writers. My own company, for the most part, was Bertie's extensive library, the curios and books left by past fellows, and a small, translucent-pink gecko who lived behind the splashback in the kitchen. Before I knew it was a gecko, it was strange tocking that I attributed to a quirk of the ancient plumbing.

The echoes of past residents carried a linear sense of community, while at the same time the faintly melancholic note of aftermath, of having missed the main event. The kitchen cupboards were cluttered with packets of paper plates left over from long-extinguished parties, half a bottle of Campari and some other sticky liquors in violent colours, the orphaned parts of appliances, a box of spices whose use-by dates had been drastically overshot. A handwritten index in a blue clothbound ledger, compiled by a poet who'd been in residence when the currency was still lire. He'd included in it tips for best coffee, cheapest haircuts, where to find Vegemite.

There was a faulty telephone that rang at odd hours with wrong numbers, or occasionally a right number, but to figure that out you really had to yell. Now and then Lorri herself would call from up the coast, Monte Argentario, and we'd exchange a few words before being thwarted by the crackly line.

One of her paintings remained in the studio, filling almost an entire wall. Shards of blues and greys summoned up an inclement sea, or an ice cavern, or a glacier, depending on the angle of light and whatever state your dreams had left you in. Closer up, the shards had soft, fibrous edges; you could see they had been torn from other paintings.

'I had a conversation with Buckminster Fuller, about triangles,' Lorri shouted down the failing telephone one day. 'It changed the way I saw things.'

I stood before the painting every morning, lost myself in it. Perhaps it changed the way I saw things. It has become very much twinned, in my mind, with the writing of Beverley Farmer.

In Bertie's library, several shelves had been set aside to hold the works of past fellows. Mythological references in the titles, so many stone faces staring out from dust jackets to signify: *here we are in the Old World.*

The cover of *The Bone House* shows one such face: an angel or death mask in close-up, wide-grained film of weathered marble. I took the book off the shelf and looked at the face and slotted it back again, several times, before finally plunging in.

It begins with a blade of light. As simple, as subtle, as that: clean winter sun shearing at the edge of a blind, sharpening in intensity before flaring into image, into meaning, like a revelatory moment in a Bergman film.

This humble phenomenon – of light transpiring to image – develops to full relevance at Farmer's elemental pace across the book's three nonlinear essays. She casts back and forth across millennia, in and out of myth: from the disparate origins of optics and everything indebted to them; to the first lenses and the findings of the first astronomers; to how we have learned to see, and our efforts to reproduce what has been seen. The epic discoveries and setbacks and losses through the light and dark ages of civilisations: time marked by menhirs and monoliths, stones that have become the fossils of their meanings; icons of reindeer graven under a cliff to call living herds to its edge; the fall of the lighthouse at Pharos; the burning of the Great Library of Alexandria and the burning of heretics; the post-Krakatoa skies of Europe, and the artists whose palettes, along with their inner weather, reflected them. Van Gogh on yellow, Goethe on red, Goethe on blue. The black bird that shadowed everything Edvard Munch saw, following a haemorrhage in his right eye.

Farmer experienced a similar shadowing (*musca volitans*) and feared, with haunting prescience, that she would one day lose her sight. This could be taken as the underlying impetus for these essays and their encyclopaedic, sometimes overwhelming breadth: the urgency to document, record, cache. The act and the art of looking, whether as writer or photographer or artist or scientist or mystic. The quixotic business of transposing this witness into language. The image hoard of one mind.

Our first job, Farmer reminds, is noticing: *The photograph has its full being in the instant of exposure. The rest is aftermath.* The text is inter-leaved with her own photographs – prints she laboured over in a makeshift darkroom in a bor-rowed shed near her home in Point Lonsdale, sealed in the light-tight, chemical interior, the sleepy sounds of hens on the other side of the wall.

There are also the embedded passages from a never-finished novel, fiction that blooms as lichen between the scrubbed bones of fact: the death of a man by a roadside in the Greek port city of Thessaloniki, and the shockwaves it casts to coastal Australia. *I see now that the story will never unfold*, Farmer cedes, after a point, though it becomes all the more indelible for that. *The meaning goes on growing, like desire, like memory, in the dark.*

The palimpsestic nature of *The Bone House*, and the mode of observation it encourages, was particularly potent in a city like Rome. Her words asked patience, but in turn bestowed the same, sharpening appreciation for both the immediate, sensory world and the histories underlain. I became enthralled by the acuity of her attention, copying passages into my notebook, gleaned from her careful gleaning:

Low tide and a waveline of jellyfish like ice on the thaw, clearer than water, so clear even the sand is alight ...

The early photographers kept a cat in the studio to act as a light meter, going by the subtle swell and shrink of its changing eyes in the changing light. How did they keep it awake?

And I went out into the Eternal City each day feeling equipped with some indefinable new apparatus for appreciating the hereto over-looked or undervalued.

Much within these essays is deeply personal – observations and desires, memories and dreams and the gauzy territory between the two. As much again, garnered, stored, housed:

> *A stored image can broadcast itself when conditions are favourable, taking form in words, in ink and paint, film, clay, stone. Images are seeds. They have latency and the power to endure. They are like stored shadows burnt on to film for a fraction of a second, decades ago, the long lost negative …*

The Bone House, published in 2005, is either a decade's work or a lifetime's, depending on how you look at it. It is the distillation of an expansive mind that seeks to delve and delve. Her tone is never didactic – rather, discursive, exploratory, delighted, unjaded, alive. To read more than a few pages at a stretch is to travel a long way from where you set out. Sometimes to travel so far as to lose the view of the mountain, only to be brought back via an unfamiliar face of it.

For a little more than a week, I read – I travelled through – very slowly. The book was there for mornings, the days drawing their shape and tone from as few as half a dozen pages. Or it was a place to come for refuge, panhandling at four a.m., unable to sleep, tilting the book towards the cheap lamp to ask, *what lasts?*

> *Relics, memorials, the tide's leavings and ours,*
> *humanity's, so few, bones and driftwood, shells,*
> *crab casts and scrawls on the sand that were*
> *wave traces ... Standing stones and rune*
> *stones, crosses, middens, ruins, shards and*

shreds as haphazard and rifted with meaning
as the elements of a dream.

Then she died. On the other side of the world. And the news of it affected me in a way that seemed unearned. A surreal plunge of loneliness, loss. A sensation like that of phantom stair – the vertiginous pitch that comes from planting a foot down somewhere you'd imagined was solid, continuous.

I had been making my way through the intricate inner logic of the essays with the sense of the author as an abiding entity, existing both within and around the text. With her death, the ground shifted. There were still the works that came before, yes. And a final book of stories, printed just in time for her to see it. But beyond that: one of her ocean-undermined escarpments, shearing off into vast sea.

This far, and no further. A familiar refrain of Farmer's throughout her writing life.

For reasons that remain elusive, I could not, at that time, finish reading the book.

SOMNAMBULANCE

Everyone carries a room about inside him. This fact can be proved by means of the sense of hearing. If someone walks fast and one pricks up one's ears and listens, say in the night, when everything round about is quiet, one hears, for instance, the rattling of a mirror not quite firmly fastened to the wall.

Franz Kafka, *The Blue Octavo Notebooks*

1987, Point Lonsdale. Each time a ship passes through the Rip, all the mirrors clatter against the walls of her weatherboard home. She wakes, if not already awake, and listens to the house thrumming in concert with the engine chugging out to sea.

One of the mirrors was quivering, aloud on the
wooden wall, and as I watched the other mirror
began and the sound reverberated in the space
between that wall and the wall of the next room,
then in the spaces of the rooms themselves ... My
bed, my body, my house were all one resonance.

The walk she takes to the lighthouse when
sleepless has the tenor of recurrent dream. Or
bewitchment, incantation, spell. *A night like that*
is wasted sleeping.

In *A Body of Water*, a writer's notebook kept
between the summers of 1987 and 1988, Farmer
revisits this same somnambulistic excursion
often enough that a reader comes to share in
her sense memory: the luminous, soaking mist
that hangs in the avenue of tea trees; the cold
rungs of the metal walkway under bare feet, or
through the thin soles of tennis shoes; the steps

lumpy with sand, and the beach steeped in dim red light cast by a pair of tide lanterns. Steam gushing in a blast from the foghorn, *so loud it was no longer sound, only pain ... I came back damp and salty at midnight, still resonating with the roar of it.*

Her characters are outsiders, foreigners, fringe dwellers. Expats and exiles, those returning home after long absences, or floundering, as callow interlopers into the close-knit cosmology of blood kin. They are novice monks, hermits, priests who will never be ordained; women biding time in shabby sublets, whose lives shrink very small while they wait for men; single mothers who have failed their children in real or imagined ways. Very often they are widows, old or young, and many of them – the people of her stories and novels – will be bound or irresistibly drawn to this particular littoral zone, lives pivoting around the cardinal point of the lighthouse, the ocean-gnawed sandstone cliffs, ears pitched to the mournful bellow of the foghorn.

She comes to know it all as intimately by night as she does by day, when she fossicks the tideline, a slight figure with pale, windblown hair, bent double over the rockpools, lost in worlds *half-hidden in this one … and mirroring, matching.*

Mirrors line the corridors of all of Farmer's writing, flashing or rippling or shattering to fragments. They are as much functional or structural devices as they are talismans, metaphors, symbols of myth and of the precariousness of translating from one language to another, one culture to another, revealing the ongoing warp of memory.

Often they are invoked as self-criticism, or self-caution:

Every tentatif *I make in the direction of a new story brings me up face to face again with the mirror. The impulse withers. What is ahead lies beyond – that is, behind – the mirror, inaccessible, invisible, unknowable. Walking forward, all I see is myself loom larger, embedded in the vista of all that is behind me.*

. . .

If my new stories can't reach into the new time, grow from the new self, better to be writing none.

A Body of Water stems in part from this anxiety: that a protracted stasis in both life and work might be more ominous than periodic dormancy, that it may signal an exhaustion, a drying up.

It opens in February 1987, on Farmer's forty-sixth birthday, with *no end in sight to the long struggle to come to terms with this isolation, this sterility.*

Two years and no stories. In the seven years prior, she has published a short novel, two story collections, numerous poems. This is her first summer in the Point Lonsdale house, where she has moved, alone, in the wake (she uses the word 'wreckage') of her marriage.

Her son, Taki, recalls the house as a refuge. Though family life was unsettled – he was mostly with his father, or at boarding school in Geelong – the township offered a comforting anonymity and privacy during the infrequent exeats he was allowed: 'We loved it there. It was a sleepy hollow then, before the holiday-house set.'

Over the year's entries, visits from Taki and close friends come as mooring lines, but otherwise the sense is of one treading water, casting about for anchorage. The task of notebook-keeping is begun in the hope that the simple and deliberate act of noticing, of drawing the immediate surrounds into language, will enact a shift in creative inertia; that fiction and poetry might spill over from the main channel of observations and reflections.

A writer's notebook. The term does so long as you allow a broad definition of the word *notebook*. The mostly undated entries are flashes of life, grist for stories and poems, interwoven with the works that do eventually crop out. There are dispatches from Buddhist retreats. Transcripts from awkward lunches and telephone arguments. A list of noms de plume she might use if she ever resorts to churning out romance novels: *Barbara Fox … Claudine Bell. How about Colleen?* Jobs she would rather do than churn out romance novels: *wash dishes again … (if any kitchen will have me).* Review notes on books, films, plays. Items from newspapers. Dreams, epiphanies, mission statements, promises. Self-admonishments as well as diligently logged criticisms from others. Flotsam, organic and not, material and not. Methods for cooking, planting, removing a green ant from a child's ear. Methods for fending off loneliness, or at least withstanding it – speculation on the elusive alchemy by which loneliness becomes the more noble solitude. Analogies for orgasms. Analogies for mist. Tide charts. No small amount of blood and candour. Intricate studies of birds, insects and sea creatures – living, dead, fossilised. A comprehensive catalogue of kelp. Intercultural comparisons of rituals, mythologies, gods. Extracts from writers, poets, philosophers: John Berger, Katherine Mansfield, Ludwig Wittgenstein, Marguerite

Duras, Janet Frame, Rainer Maria Rilke. She is proficient in several languages, and when quoting works in translation will often include two or more versions along with the original text, deliberations on which is the truer, the more artful – *Bly's 'fresh' is a false note there; and 'that dies' sounds as if it's in the process of dying.* Her fastidious concern for accuracy as well as authenticity, for the evolutions of language in all its slipperiness, is present throughout much of her writing. The endless opportunities for misunderstanding, for being misunderstood.

D.H. Lawrence figures among Farmer's most prominent touchstones, and the lines she includes from *Studies in Classic American Literature* seem to strike directly at the heart of things: *Sometimes snakes can't slough. They can't burst their old skin. Then they go sick and die inside the old skin, and nobody ever sees the new pattern*. Another way of saying: *change or die*.

From Octavio Paz she gains reassurance that stasis is a necessary condition for writing, that *sterility precedes inspiration, as emptiness precedes plenitude. The poetic word crops out after periods of drought*. She considers: *Maybe an anxious rigidity about forms is part of the problem. Work on that assumption for the time being. Just write on without worrying what it is I'm writing. Trusting to instinct, letting it evolve*.

A Body of Water is the first time she has written place from within it. Before this, she has written 1950s Melbourne from a village in Greece; Greek village life following her return to Australia; America once the inciting events were *closed off in time and place and quite remote*. This notebook is, among other things, an attempt at being avidly present, planting life alongside practice to encourage a symbiosis rich enough to provoke not only new works, but new ways of working, new ways of seeing. To return to Lawrence's snake: to be fresh and thinly skinned, alive to element. Susceptible.

In the year of 1987 Farmer digs down, figuratively and literally, putting hands and roots into the loamy coastal earth, in a bid for sturdier mooring. She plants a dormant Black Genoa fig in the garden *in the hope that one will bear fruit here, even in this dry sand: This is the first fruit tree I – I alone – have ever planted in my life! But that wasn't the reason that I felt, there on my knees, that I was making an offering in the mud that I had opened for its roots.*

In thirty years, the Black Genoa will have surpassed her hopes of it growing roof-tall.

~

There are people – I've known some of them – who are not continuously shadowed by whatever life they are not living, the version (or versions) they chose against. I have no idea what that must be like. It's so alien a concept that I don't even know if I ought to envy it. In reading *A Body of Water*, I recognise too well the sabotaging compulsion to constant comparison, *this* to *that*, *there* to *here*, a head cramped with contrasting clocks. And while Tomas Tranströmer's poems never appear in *A Body of Water* (though I keep checking to be certain), my reading of it is inflected with lines from his poem 'The Blue House': *I am grateful for this life! And yet I miss the alternatives.* Gratitude for the present, in Farmer's text, seems to come by sheer force of will, while longing for elsewhere – that restlessness of intellect and voracity for travel – arrives as a natural state of being.

Reckonings with the past are endemic to the notebook genre, and while in *A Body of Water* the forward momentum is bound to the turn of tides and seasons in this coastal township, the heightened colour of remembered lives flashes through, the present given dimension by all that came before. The northern village of Polypetron, where Farmer lived with her husband and his family, is conjured by ordinary daily sensations: a sullen sky, fig-splitting heat or the thud of windfall apples into dead leaves; glossy mountains of chestnuts or the red chainmail of fish scales. It shimmers up in the undefended territory of dreams, and in the peel of the passing bell: *I hardly ever hear it here; not like Polypetron, where the church was one street away and funerals would trail in the dust past our house, women wailing with their swathed heads flung back.*

Greek attitudes towards life and death hold significant fascination for Farmer. She grew up an only child in 1950s suburban Melbourne, in a household where emotions were not discussed, sensitive explanations indefinitely deferred – austerities she broke from as soon as she could, hitchhiking to Sydney at eighteen and hopping a cargo ship to Tahiti with a pocket-sized book of Gauguin's prints. Once in rural Greece, despite her introversion, she revelled in the sense of close-knit community, first as a young bride and then as a new mother. 'I think she really loved the whole "it takes a village to raise a child" vibe of it all,' says Taki.

There was also the nearness of myth, flush up against the everyday. Household gods who took the form of snakes and other creatures; emissaries from the afterlife; the soul manifesting as a moth, a bee, a flame. *The past walks at night all over the earth, but in Greece in broad day-light.* Traditions and superstitions to observe or else risk offence. The rituals and lore surrounding mourning, and the spirited, demonstrative expressions of grief, all in stark contrast to the muted, deflective Australian counterpart.

A tableau, from the unfinished novel nested within *The Bone House*:

The bed smells of hay and something acrid and sweet, wine in the basin. Two women are hovering over the doughy mass on the bed, one a darkness, his mother, and the other in a rim of yellow. One lifts the scrubby grey head in both hands while the other fastens a bandage under the chin, knotting it at the nape. He hears the soft lick and slop of the sponge as they lift one limp arm and then the other, one leg and the other, a line of drips as yellow as oil strung out

shimmering. He is as cold as the sea. The strokes
of the sponge leave a varnish of water scribbled
with black hairs.

To Rilke, death is simply the *side of life that
is turned away from us.* Farmer tends to accord
death the same exacting attention she does life –
observing with a philosophical, almost painterly
acuity. A washed-up seal pup, *fingerbones like
rosary beads*, or a seabird, with its *fretty* neck,
is viewed with the same curiosity as a moth –
bent amber feeler, a sumptuous ruff – or tree bark,
sunlight, a spider:

*A huntsman spider came in the moment the
power failed, a monster of shadow flickering on
the wall – I hit and killed it with a broom … It
went small, clenched on the carpet like a crab in
sand – red-brown and translucent. I should have*

drawn its corpse. Attended to its intricacies.
That might be a way of learning to tolerate these
agile, springing creatures. They're not furtive,
not savage like funnel-webs, they don't weave a
furry hole and crouch in it. They have a young,
wild gallantry about them. Leggy desperadoes.

The intricacies have been attended to, all the same. A creature study whose predecessors might be encountered in the essays of Virginia Woolf or Annie Dillard.

In reading Farmer, I'm often put in mind of Dillard. Both writers share a capacity for exactitude drawn at an emotional remove – what might be mistaken for detached observation. However, while there may often be a lack of sentimentality regarding death, there's never a lack of wonder.

A few years ago, I sent a friend a passage

from Dillard's essay 'The Death of the Moth', which describes the eponymous death (accidental, by candle flame). *The wax rose in the moth's body from her soaking abdomen to her thorax to the jagged hole where her head should be, and widened into flame, a saffron-yellow flame that robed her to the ground like any immolating monk.* His response threw me: *cold, cruel, clinical.* An unwitting echo of another of Dillard's famously observed deaths, in 'The Deer at Providencia', which vivisects the male gaze on the female gaze, what it expects and accepts as *female.* The author observes a trussed deer awaiting slaughter outside a small Ecuadorian village, while the fellow North Americans on her tour group, all men, observe her, appraising her lack of expression: *I looked detached, apparently, or hard, or calm, or focussed, still. I don't know. I was thinking.* Her travelling companions are either awed or unnerved by her demeanour, which they view as unfeminine: *If it had been my wife ...*

Gentlemen of the city, Dillard asks in the essay, after the fact, *what surprises you? That there is suffering here, or that I know it?*

Here the two modes of witness diverge. Unlike Dillard, Farmer cannot stand by to animal suffering, which is beyond her considerable powers of translation. Her discomfort with the *process* of dying is such that she usually does turn away.

Otherwise, on either side of that threshold, Farmer's attention is unstinting. Her attendance to intricacies, be they of spiderwebs or the shadows of spiderwebs or webs of light through water – she is egalitarian in the designation of worthiness. The lengthy descriptions of water and creature and stone. Those atomising, anatomising meditations on microcosmic significance that zero in on barb and pore and grain … It's true that some days, I do not have the patience with which to meet her patience. Have come to think of a surfeit of patience, in women, as near enough to fatal.

Sandstone is honeycomb in this still afternoon sun, pitted with swallows' nests. All this beach is the same colour – sand, rock and rockpool. The small mouse-shrieks of swallows skim and soar. The wave-shaped, whale-shaped headland is dark in the spray of the western sky. Into the eastern sky a ship surges from behind the light-house, trailing a smoke blur. Its surfaces flash. A point like a star pierces the masthead. My foot-prints flatten the crisp arrowheads left by gulls. At the high tide mark, along the hairline of the marram grass, clumps of feathers, all hollowed out, clench empty beaks and claws.

Yes, but after a point, a reader wants to know: *when* are we getting to the story?

By this we mean: the human story. Which is the great isolating sadness and destructive solipsism of our time. When we read as if the human story were the *only* story – dismissing the natural world as merely setting or backdrop, as if we were not intricately interwoven with other beings and scales of time – we are missing much of the point.

This comes as nothing new to Indigenous ways of knowing, and of telling, which more readily make allowance for sentience in forms non-Indigenous writers are typically less inclined to recognise.

This awareness of interdependency often figures in integrative, interdisciplinary frameworks. Stories are told – are carried, sustained, exchanged – through more ways than simply the written, the spoken, or even the sung word; more ways than the human-made mark or image. Appreciating this, when working within the confines of text, of language, certain formal boundaries come to seem counterproductive, inhibitive, even disingenuous.

Over the past few years, concurrent to our slow-dawning recognition of accelerated ecological decline, there is increasing hunger for narratives that do more than simply reflect the human story back to us. Narratives that are not, or not entirely, anthropocentric. The architects of the old stories, the myth-makers, knew this, but we stand in need of constant reminding.

In *A Body of Water*, Farmer quotes from Dōgen's *Shōbōgenzō*:

> *Students cannot gain enlightenment simply because they retain their preconceptions. Without*

knowing who taught them these things, they consider the mind to be thought and perceptions and do not believe it when they are told that the mind is plants and trees.

It's a sensibility that lends itself to hybrid, non-linear modes of storytelling. In the present moment, narrative forms that reorient the way we relate to our environment are critical in renewing our responsibility to it.

Farmer's final realist story, 'A Ring of Gold', was written over the decades following her first year in the shuddering Point Lonsdale house. By virtue of her close attention to this place over thirty years, the Bellarine Peninsula emerges not merely as setting, or even *character* (help us), but rather as what it is: an evolving and eroding ecosystem, as susceptible to human influence as it is a determining force on the lives of those who inhabit it.

Its narrator, an older widow whose sensibilities resemble something of Farmer's, combs the same stretch of coast with an attention honed by decades of looking, recording from the same vantage the immanence of loss or threat:

> *At new moon and full moon, high tides have always ravaged this southern shore, back beach and front beach alike, and this year the last of the winter king tides has been dragging on into September, in the wake of the spring equinox. Storms and dark days of heavy swell have sent the waves smashing over the bluestone seawall, breaching it, flooding; a slab of the cliff face has slid off overnight, cracked in half like a biscuit; the little wooden pier by the lighthouse has kept disappearing, lurching, reappearing from under a weight of water; and the ocean swell always*

licking away at the dunes has been wolfing them
down lately, undermining them.

Much is playing out here, in plain view, but on a longer and larger scale than most of us have the lens for.

Yes, some days I find it difficult to meet her patience with the same. Other days, I feel it working on me, in the way that Berger or Dillard or Woolf work on me, recalibrating my capacity for presence, my sense of time and scale, a sensitivity to place.

In the early 2000s, Californian soundscape ecologists Bernie Krause and Stuart Gage developed a vocabulary for the way we hear and interpret any natural soundscape. The 'geo-phony' refers to the elemental, non-biological sounds of a wild environment, the first noise on the planet – weather, water in all its forms, the clatter of pebbles raked across a shoreline by a receding wave. The 'biophony' concerns the sounds that all non-human animals produce within a habitat. The 'anthropophony' is us: our voices, our music, along with everything we have engineered – all of our highways and flight paths and heavy industry.

Within this system, Krause's theory of 'acoustic niche' describes how all creatures within a healthy biome find a unique bandwidth in which to iterate or vocalise, 'just like instruments in an orchestra'. If that distinct register is subsumed (by human-introduced noise, for instance), they're unable to transmit and receive, which means they're unable to effectively mate, hunt, caution – to engage in many of the behaviours necessary to existence.

As the anthropophony crescendoes to an unprecedented volume, creatures who communicate within certain bandwidths are being drowned out, edged away. In up to two-thirds of the 1200 to 1300 biomes Krause has recorded around the world over the past five decades – many of them once remote – the biophony has been rendered unrecognisable, or altogether silent: 'The transformation caused by human endeavour has been so complete and so abrupt even the birds are speechless.'

(*Nature's old song and dance*, as Dillard puts it, *the show we drove from town*.)

From animals we learned music, we learned dance. I've come to think of these biophonic vanishings (which go unnoticed by most of us) as an analogue of the threat of long-reaching loneliness with which we are faced. It's the stuff of hubristic tragedy – to be left here trembling within our own frequency, humming along to our own self-referential song.

'The cure for loneliness is solitude,' Marianne Moore told America's sixteen-year-olds in 1958, and the rest of us introspective crowd-shirkers have been reciting it ever since, if neatly snipping it away from its religious context. But also leaving off, more regrettably, Moore's urging that 'one should, above all, learn to be silent, to listen'.

Does sustained attentiveness depend upon prolonged stretches of solitude? Certainly it depends upon protracted silence, and sustained, non-threatening silence in the company of another is a rare-enough state of grace, even with those we love.

Those who knew Beverley Farmer, whether intimately or at a remove, are swift to recall her extreme shyness, a social discomfort that was as painful to witness as it must have been to inhabit. A fastidious need for precision in expression, her own most of all, would sometimes cause her to freeze into silence (and, in extremis, to destroy her unsatisfactory manuscripts). Like many photographers, she much preferred to stay on the taking side of the lens. She was slight and softly spoken, unassuming in stature and in manner. A warm but cautious architect of boundaries, across relationships, one who might slip away from gatherings without a goodbye.

When I consider what separates her from writers like Annie Dillard or Anne Carson – with whom she shares so many concerns, approached through similarly peripatetic lines of enquiry – what it comes down to is wryness. Sardonicism is a form of social armour; Farmer seems never to have acquired it.

But her writing, especially in *A Body of Water*, is punctured by a striking candour that catches a reader off-guard, razes any presumption that equates introversion with meekness or dispassion: *I hardly slept. At about sunrise I woke and gave myself five orgasms. After the first one, as happens often now, I melted into hot tears: this slow trickle across my cheeks down into my ears was so like a tongue, two tongues, that the lust kept welling up again and was exhausted by the end rather than assuaged.*

I think of Alice Munro's fiction – a reader may think she's settled in a demure domestic milieu when all of a sudden, someone's elderly mother blows it to bits by listing into the particulars of a wistfully remembered orgy.

There was also a physical boldness, almost a recklessness, in the way Farmer inhabited her solitude. Her discomfort in crowds and of public attention had its counterparts in the lust for experience and the confidence with which she moved though the world anonymously. The moonless walks through the tea trees to the Point Lonsdale lighthouse echo the late-night missions of her teens, cycling to the West Melbourne docks with camera in hand, to shoot long exposures of ships, the reflections of lights dripping in the black water. (*Who but a* hore *goes to the docks alone?* a Greek lover demands in notes for an unfinished story.)

If she was lonely, that year, she made functional use of that loneliness, in the manner celebrated by abstract impressionist Agnes Martin: *If you're alone you're focussing on every-thing – you're just affected by everything; the sky and the wind and the air. Nature, all of nature. And you're responding one hundred percent.*

A Body of Water is, ultimately, as much an

effort at sounding the contours of solitude as it is a means of overcoming creative impasse. She quotes from May Sarton's *Journal of a Solitude*: *It occurs to me that boredom and panic are the two devils the solitary must combat.*

The distinction between solitude and loneliness has a lot to do with agency. In 1987 Farmer is more isolated than she would choose to be. Greece, and the way of life there – vividly conveyed in her first story collection, *Milk* – is no longer available to her in the same way. In recurrent dreams of her former husband's village, she goes unrecognised. *No one remembered, no one had ever heard of me.*

How to appreciate the higher attributes of solitude without succumbing to the boredom and panic? She is in the early years of Buddhist practice, regularly attending teachings in Melbourne and venturing on interstate retreats, and the influence of Buddhist tenets is palpable. (Of the year's yield – half a dozen stories – the first and final draw from her nascent immersion in Buddhism. 'A Drop of Water', which breaks her two-year 'drought', begins irresistibly: *Tenzin who used to be Hans ...*) It seems little wonder that she might find solace in the precepts of noble detachment at this juncture in her life – the possibility of making something grander, self-determining, of self-estrangement. A redefining of loss as a step on the graduated path. By the end of *A Body of Water*, Farmer's chronicle of a year of creative stasis and solitude proves, through the act of writing, a means of traversing both.

On a morning following her forty-seventh birthday, she wakes from a dream of dining alone:

I went to his new restaurant, an outsider; none of the waitresses hurrying up and down the wooden stairs knew me. A great olive tree spread roof-high by the door, dripping black olives, luminous black and as large as plums. I broke off sprigs from three branches and took them inside; there I put them in a glass bowl which immediately brimmed green with oil, the leaves and the olives floating up, magnified. *Oh, you had no right to do that!* someone said. I planted this tree, *I answered, waking.*

WAYFARING

*All experience has its meaning beyond the
moment, a meaning which is only ever gradually revealed and grows with the revelation.
The process is always incomplete. The meaning goes on growing, like desire, like memory,
in the dark. The fullness of the meaning is
only to be known by its weight, its power of
displacement.*

Beverley Farmer, *The Bone House*

*T*he Bone House is at once a work of rest-
less genius and of unshakeable focus.
And astonishingly few seem to have
read it. This overlooking leaves me discouraged
about what carries in Australian literature, what

else, *who* else, might be slipping from rightful notice.

In *A Body of Water*, Farmer writes of Marjorie Barnard: *It matters very much to me, the invisible network of women reading each other's work and cherishing it.*

I adore these lines, but at the same time, they cannot date quickly enough.

As to whether a male writer might have enjoyed more recognition for the same kind of innovatory feat, there's a relevant case to be made, but I'm tired just thinking about it. Chalk me up as a *yes*, and let us move on. I want to use these pages to speak to the work itself.

We could approach the genre-eliding structure of *The Bone House* as cache, storehouse, memoryhouse – indeed, a bone house, an ossuary. Farmer intended it as a 'commonplace book', a practice that dates at least as far back as the Pax Romana (Marcus Aurelius's *Meditations* is an example). The governing conceit of such books is the collation of knowledge or thought on any given subject or subjects – a curation of information, as distinct from a diary, though diary-like entries might appear amid quotations, illustrations, commentaries. *Commonplace* suggests a way of reading, concerned as it is with the collation of knowledge, rather than its bestowal. And while in Farmer's case there must have come, at some point in the process of compilation, the intent to publish for an audience (as we sometimes detect in suspiciously eloquent diaries), it remains an intimate and idiosyncratic pursuit.

As a published work, the commonplace book takes a modest, open-handed position: *Here is what I found; you may make something different of it.* The underlying structure – the story – is that of the author-curator's fascination: the ambit of their curiosity and the terrain it leads them through. It's a celebration of wayfaring, of intellectual wanderlust. Narrative transpires in the going, on the hoof, and the light tangent or shunpike might become an expedition; might prove the destination.

Farmer's commentary in *The Bone House* is rarely overt, and exists largely through proximity and pause, as in the essays of Eliot Weinberger: the quiet, almost stoical accrual of detail that gradually flares to broader significance, illuminations that occur within the mind of the reader, rather than on the page. Both Farmer and Weinberger become familiar to the reader by their cognitive gait, by how and where they roam, what the eye lights and lingers on, their peregrinations and patterns of return. Such writers are often just as audible in their seismic Unsaids.

Narrative here is the act of pursuit, a desire to get *at the root of things* by one who knows there is no single source, but a sprawling, infinitely interwoven system that stretches out to encompass cultures and epochs, empires continuous and broken and lost. We might start in the Cyclades with the Minoan eruption of Thera and arrive centuries later at a fjord in Norway, the skies tinted volcanic by the far-flung ash of Krakatoa, a young Edvard Munch trembling against a railing – the genesis of one of the most iconic artworks of the nineteenth century:

I was walking along the road with two friends. The sun set. I felt a tinge of melancholy. Suddenly the sky became a bloody red.

I stopped, leaned against the railing, dead tired and I looked at the flaming clouds that

hung like blood and a sword over the blue-black
fjord and city.

My friends walked on. I stood there, trem-
bling with fright. And I felt a loud, unending
scream piercing nature.

En route, we have encountered the buried harbour town of Akrotiri, cocooned in ash four centuries before the Trojan War, its frescoes later painstakingly reconstructed from ash-sealed fragments; the myth-cloaked megaliths jutting up throughout Europe; the origins and numinous properties of stones (*Amber is variously the tears shed into the river Po every year by nymphs turned into poplar trees … elsewhere it is lynx urine petrified*); the Neolithic ruins and black-veiled witch queens of Orkney; ancient traditions of beekeeping; the fates of Viking fleets; and contemporary passage across the Arctic Circle

(*How do you live a life where there is one long day in a year, the summer, the unsetting sun, and one long winter night?*). It is a work whose way is desire lines and parch marks, over anything like a paved thoroughfare, and when I come back to it in five years, or again in ten years, I'll no doubt sight entirely different cairns and beacons.

For now, what I'm moved to return to are *apparitions*, *semblances*, *shades*: the surprisingly widespread and enduring belief that both the psyche and the corporeal self are a series of infinitely overlaid transparencies. Farmer tracks this belief across centuries and various schools of thought, through optics, art and philosophy. *Membranes*, *husks*, *veils*, *impressions* – the language varies, but the concept is fundamentally the same: layers we shed involuntarily, or which are torn away through the very act of being looked at. The air around us swarming with these invisible simulacra stripped from our outermost selves. These same shades might steal into our sleep as dreams or terrors.

To photograph was to capture one of these semblances. Emily Dickinson was said to loathe her daguerreotype, while Balzac feared the Daguerreian operation would strip away a layer of the self. The idea persists in our language: we take photographs, have our photographs taken – even if photography is no longer, generally speaking, an alchemy.

Roland Barthes, too, was uneasy with being a subject, *a micro-version of death (of parenthesis): I am truly becoming a spectre*. But as a viewer, he was more inclined towards the splendour of this process, writing of the photograph as *literally an emanation of the referent* that reaches across time and space *like the delayed rays of a star*.

Farmer's ongoing fascination with artists 'possessed' recurs throughout *The Bone House*, along with the often arbitrary diagnostics that distinguish genius (in its ancient meaning: a kind of benevolent possession or guidance) from mental illness. She writes of Woolf's and Rilke's respective efforts to subdue or invoke their demons and angels: *Rilke would recoil from the thought of treatment to rid him of his devils – his angels might leave him too.* She goes on: *How might Gauguin have chosen? How might van Gogh?* But it is Munch, unwitting icon of twentieth-century melancholia, said to have died with a copy of Dostoyevsky's *The Possessed* in his lap, who she stands in the strongest light: *his black angels were his devils, they would be the death of him. Treatment, even shock treatment, might keep them at bay. Munch had chosen life.*

In 1961, at age twenty, Farmer's nascent teaching career was forestalled when the breakdown that followed the end of her first significant relationship was diagnosed as schizophrenia. Deemed unfit for teaching, she worked a string of hospitality jobs to repay her teaching bond. This was same era of psychiatry that also saw Janet Frame misdiagnosed and institutionally punished for depressive episodes. In Beverley Farmer's case, the diagnosis may have had a lot to do with systemic homophobia.

Farmer's debut novel, *Alone*, was published in 1980 but had a much longer genesis, first appearing as a story published in *Westerly* in 1968, when she was twenty-seven. Its protagonist, Shirley, admonishes herself for loving a woman. She asks, *Do people somehow sense that I'm abnormal?* At the state library in Melbourne, she hunches over Freud and Jung and Adler,

books on abnormal psychology and sexual per-
versions that heighten her sense of alienation.

In *A Body of Water*, written in her late forties,
Farmer addresses her longstanding discomfit
with the novel: 'I've felt embarrassed for a long
time about *Alone*, but I need to acknowledge it
as mine.' There is an almost familial responsibility 'not to deny and reject my Shirley'.

Within the notebook, she revisits her first
and most formative relationship in a far more
grateful light:

> to have had my first experience of love in the
> arms of a woman was a blessing. I see it as a
> blessing. To have been known in my own body
> and to have known hers, before ever turning to
> encounter a man ... One more year will make
> it thirty years ago and I can still remember and
> will remember for ever the look of her lying

with me, her eyes closed, her breasts against
mine and our thighs entwined, my hands in her
hair, all that warm abundance and security. To
love her (or anyone) in the desperate way I loved
her, that was the mistake, not the lovemaking,
which was sane and strong – at first, anyway –
and has stood me in good stead.

Sane, she affirms, perhaps still felt the need to affirm. I cannot read that word without wanting to tear something to pieces. For all the hurt it intones, and all the waste.

In the initial telling of 'Alone', she tried to write the lover as a man – 'I thought it would be a lot easier for people to accept the story,' she said in a 1994 interview – but felt it insincere. She'd never slept with a man, at that point. 'I wasn't interested in writing the story if I had to fake it that much.'

She told the interviewer, Marylynn Scott, that she wasn't surprised by readers conflating her with her characters. 'But I feel invaded by it.'

Within Farmer's notebook entries, some of the frank intimacies – emotional, bodily, psychological – may have the ring of exposure or confession (though such a read might be led by the bizarre perpetuation, in literature, of a parallel universe where women don't bleed – except by violence, as plot points). As to deeper, more closely guarded truths, a reader senses there are certain revelations she prefers to approach obliquely, through the experiences of fictionalised others: *Weaving my way is the only way I can go. Sidetrack to sidetrack snakewise and if I wear out my skin I will have to shuck it.*

Within *The Bone House*, Edvard Munch emerges not only as a compelling model of vision and artistry, but as something of a catalyst. At times she voices – inhabits – his interior with a similar fluidity to Sebald in *The Emigrants*, seamlessly dissolving the boundaries between author and subject, a wash between consciousnesses:

> *The face is a blank, lit or unlit, the mirror face under the shine holds nothing but silence. It is wordless. There are no words to put to this face. He puts the palms of both hands to it, clamps it between them because it is so lacking all solidity, a face as it might be reflected in slowly moving water …*

Then:

Once, one day, I am a madwoman. More than once.

Day after day, Farmer writes,

I am no more than a skin in a mirror, paper-thin on the silver, mute, the ghost of a self. Life is a matter of lying in bed outlining in ink on the body a hand, another hand and two feet ... tracing each ridge and crease, the groove around each nail, the fan of bones and the ravels of veins ...

Madwoman. If not for this, the scene could read just as easily as further blurring of author and subject, another kind of similitude, another kind of possession. But she swivels the lamp, passes the mirror.

Either way – as artist or writer – the nulled self might emerge from that harrowing state of non-being through the deliberate act of attention, composition; line after line of painstaking articulation, until *solid hands, and solid feet,* now convincing, might bear their owner out on all fours.

OPEN SWIMMER

Is the first time something ever happens to you imprinted for good? Why do our earliest memories last the longest, as if having had longer to embed themselves made all the difference?

Beverley Farmer, 'A Ring of Gold'

I n the later years of her life and practice, French sculptor Louise Bourgeois emptied out all her wardrobes and linen chests of the clothing she knew she would never wear again – the dresses and shirts and skirts and stockings and slips – along with tablecloths, sheets, blankets and quilts amassed over decades. These became the primary materials for her later works.

(Or, we could say that life was the primary material, and these lived-in fabrics a perfect medium, years and events permeating the fibres, traces of past selves ghosting through the warp and weft.)

Bourgeois had gained an intimate authority with textiles early in life, in the workshop of her family's tapestry restoration business, where she was recruited from age twelve to draw in the patterns of damaged or missing sections. Her most iconic sculptures – the immense bronze and steel spiders that crouch between eight and thirty feet to fill whole rooms or tower at entryways of major galleries – pay tribute to this heritage. The outwardly menacing spiders are in fact an affectionate homage to her mother: the clever and subtle weaver, the patient and protective restorer.

The 1997 sculpture *Blue Days* is a quieter evocation of this legacy: an armature with seven garments hung in stilled orbit around a red-glass nucleus, shirts and dresses and slips in various shades of blue, draped upon or clinging to soft forms of a body (her body?) at varying stages of life.

The clothes bear intimate testament to the phases of life they've been worn through: in the small accommodations of taking up or in, letting out or down; in the accidental or incidental marked in the tiny, near-invisible sutures; in the stains and frayed edges, the patches worn sheer. All evidence of transformations wrought over years or in instants, and open to interpretation. One might look and wonder, *Was that hunger, dearth, pregnancy, plenty, recklessness, fun, modesty, thrift, grief, gratitude, custodianship, affection ...?*

The Waiting Hours, created a decade later, is composed of richer materials less redolent of daily life. It is a series of twelve small oceanscapes – Bourgeois called them 'fabric drawings' – sewn from blue, black, pink and grey silk. Over the sequence, the sky, blue and unremarkable in the first panel, becomes a segmented pinwheel; the perspective shifts, tilts, the ocean ebbs and rises, the horizon dips and drops away, the atmosphere lours until the distinction between sky and sea is lost. At last there is only the darkening whorl around the small white axis of a singular source of light shrunk to a pinhole – this could be the moon, but the geometry of the outward radiating lines make it seem less a heavenly object and more a lacuna, a blink through to some blinding unknown, at once a pivot point and a vanishing point.

I first saw *The Waiting Hours* at the Heide gallery, on Melbourne's outskirts, in 2013, amid the crush and murmur of a closing-day crowd. Even so. Its effect on me was one of powerful undercurrent. I felt not much and then, abruptly, disconsolate. Swept out of depth. A plunge, a plummet: the inrush towards that oceanic sense of recognition experienced most commonly in dreams, but sometimes spilling over into waking life – encounters in art and music, in nature or, more rarely, in meeting (as though *hello, again*). Occasionally it comes free of any obvious catalyst. The fleeting glimpse of the underlying pattern showing through, when we feel we see clearly, or are clearly seen.

Virginia Woolf spoke of it as a welcome or valuable shock – sometimes a dreadful, destabilising one – and suspected it was the capacity to receive such shocks that made her a writer. (*Now and again we rise to the surface and that is what you see us by.*)

Janet Frame said it was like seeing *the invisible beyond the real*. An echo of Rilke – whether intentional or subconscious – whose *Sonnets to Orpheus* had sustained her through her time in the Seacliff asylum.

Annie Dillard – ever winking between worldly mysticism and worldly cynicism – pulled it to all sorts of exquisite pieces. Among the sharpest: *It is like something you memorised once and forgot. Now it comes back and rips away your breath.*

More recently Louise Erdrich, while eloquently fending off a designation of magic realism, offered that there are times *where there seems to be some kind of emotional barrier that's down and you see things. When coincidences aren't coincidences. When everything is charged with meaning and dreams are predictive and real and hard to distinguish from reality.*

As a response to art, this collapsing of barriers comes when as readers or viewers or listeners we feel we are laid open to a pure understanding of artistic intent – not only the words or the image or the music but whatever force is at work behind it. The underswell lofting us up for an instant; or something cold down there in the collective dark, brushing an ankle. A moment of recognition you understand will sound out across your life, and will build to greater resonance, greater significance, down the years.

On the way to the Bourgeois exhibition with my then husband, I had worried that we couldn't afford the admission. We were packing down our lives to move to Canada, for which I'd drastically underestimated the cost.

Patrick, in his usual quiet wisdom, that sees the value of art above almost all else: 'In five, ten years' time, you won't remember whatever else we would've spent the money on. But you'll remember this.'

Somehow, it's only in writing this that I realise the connection, the common elements between Louise Bourgeois' *The Waiting Hours* and Lorri Whiting's untitled painting in the Rome studio, where I first encountered *The Bone House* – the stirring of a deep awareness, the barest shadow of an underlying pattern, the confluence of loss and coherence.

The long story that opens Beverley Farmer's final collection reads as a distillation of all her life's concerns. (We have already met, in brief, the beachcombing protagonist who shares so many of the author's traits and tendencies: her elemental attention, her love of ocean swimming, her impressive vocabulary for seaweed.)

In 'A Ring of Gold', it is the dog days of summer in a coastal town besieged by holiday-makers. The unnamed protagonist has been alone, widowed so long she can barely remember her husband's face, unless in dreams. She keeps time in the tides, the boom of the foghorn, the passing bell on Sundays, the Antarctic wind that flays the roof iron. Living lightly, *on the surface and in the shallows of the present moment.* There is a sense throughout of finitude, and of one preparing to make peace with it.

One morning, a bull seal appears on the surf beach, the first living seal she has seen on a shore known since childhood. *Fluid, wire-whiskered, blind, monumental, the seals sits and shakes his water off. He bends himself to scratch and sends more spray flying out with his flipper, which is a long-boned hand of bronze, she sees. A mailed hand. Where is the blood? She can't see any.*

A throng of gawkers surrounds the seal, steadily pressing in, half curious, half taunting, until the creature rears up in a long and silent roar, before convulsing back towards the ocean, vanishing out beyond the Rip.

The crowd scatters, all but the woman, who is *rigid, open-mouthed with shock. Before her eyes the salmon-red gullet of the seal bared in a mute, mutual scream of horrified recognition.*

In a nod to the selkie myth – both foundation and touchstone for Farmer, most at the fore in her 1992 novel *The Seal Woman* – the apparition and disapparition of the seal is treated as a form of summons.

Across Farmer's works, there has always been an attraction to those beings who occupy two realms, above and below, water and earth. Once one has lived elsewhere, lived differently, it doesn't matter whether she stays to forge a new life or turns back towards the old, or moves on once again; there will always be the shadow, the after-image, of the life not lived.

'A Ring of Gold' is another palimpsest; a briefer, early version of it was published in 1995, in the journal *Kunapipi*. In the collection *This Water* it has been returned to, shaken out and remade – the final days of a final summer let out to accommodate all that surfaces from deep early memory, with disorienting clarity and immediacy, at the winding out of a life: childhood's victories and losses, injuries and epiphanies; the artefacts one sees, from a late vantage, as fundamental to the fabric of a self. The red bathers that made it easy for her parents to spot her in the waves, a custom carried into adulthood. The books that brought the greater world into her tiny corner of it. The blood that arrived each month, barring her from the water – her element – for reasons that were never made clear: *was it in case sharks could smell the blood?*

Learning to swim, learning to read.

Learning shame, and – much more slowly, over time – unlearning it.

Farmer wrote the stories in *This Water* knowing they would be her last. Parkinson's is an unpredictable but progressive disorder: the onset and severity of symptoms differ from person to person. She had suspected the diagnosis for years, before physicians finally confirmed it. By then she had four or five working years ahead of her, and she took these for all they were worth, writing against elapsing light, literally and figuratively, as her vision diminished and motor function and mental energy deteriorated.

'A Ring of Gold' reads as a sifting through the alluvial miscellany built up at an estuary, the outflow of force as well as all that is swept along on it. *Who am I, coming back into being in this tight skin each morning? At the time of waking, anyone, no one. Where am I, she thinks, until it dawns. And how old? All the ages she has ever been.*

Midway through, the woman takes stock of her decades of fossicking from shore walks: *the whelks and earshells and crab casts, the rosy cuttlebone with its white hood, the stubbled sea urchin, the seabird skull on its fretwork of neck, the crab nipper inkwashed blue, the chunk of jade green bottle glass.* At this point in the story, a reader appreciates this litany as a form of ontological reflection – a whelk is a waystation somewhere between oblivion and limestone.

To these she adds a plain gold ring, a man's wedding band, found upon the sand. It was dutifully handed to police but returned to her when unclaimed, in an envelope inscribed *one gold coloured Ring*.

This archive of keepsaking is among the later additions to the story. Others resonate with a sense of waiting, of threshold and captivity, and the final version is freighted with this biding. The leitmotif of a ship clamped in pack ice, its crew of Antarctic expeditioners vaulted in the oily light of blubber lanterns, awaiting the spring thaw; a Portuguese library closed off to readers *as if under a vow of silence*:

> *The inhabitants are librarians and silverfish and bats like ghosts, skeletal, almost transparent, no bigger than moths, that live on the silverfish. At twilight they wake up for the hunt, weaving their flight paths, flitting and chittering, swooping down in whirlpools of dust. At closing*

time the librarians cover the tables to catch the
droppings. In the morning they clean up ... This
library is its own ghost, a real library in a city
and a living fairy tale, or myth, or fable.

The other four stories in *This Water* are snow-bound, stone-bound, swan-bound, sounding deeper into lore, which influenced so much of Farmer's reading and writing, her lens for the world. All are retellings, Celtic, French and Greek myths, sagas, folk stories, fairytales: the pursuit of Diarmuid and Gráinne ('This Water'), the children of Lir ('The Blood Red of Her Silks'), Clytemnestra and Agamemnon ('Tongue of Blood'), Bluebeard ('The Ice Bride').

These stories enact many kinds of entrapment, bewitchment, transmutation – restorations and reprieves that come centuries too late. Her heroines endure indefinite waiting, sometimes in vain, sometimes to their liberation. The swan siblings in 'The Blood Red of Her Silks' are restored to human form after 900 years of flight, but as lifeless bundles of dust and bone.

All could be considered expat myths of one kind or another – stories of exile, or self-estrangement, occasionally of return, with the caveat: *You cannot step into the same river twice; you can't go home again.*

Many writers, late in their piece, circle back to mythology – be it in the lore passed down through cultural memory, or those sites, images and experiences of childhood that over time take on an allegorical significance, become suffused with the gravity of fate.

Yasunari Kawabata returned to the very short form, his palm-of-the-hand stories, in which he was most given to parable. The last of these, 'Gleanings from Snow Country', written a few months before his death, is a compression of his best-known work, *Snow Country*, and a means of return to Echigo-Yuzawa, where he lived while composing it thirty years earlier.

Rilke wrote *Sonnets to Orpheus* in an *act of breathless obedience*, in memory of a friend's young daughter, but speaking more largely to the boundlessness of time and our wash in it, *incessantly flowing over and over to those who preceded us and to those who apparently come after us.* He understood that in these, together with the *Duino Elegies*, his life's work was done.

In the opening lines of *The Lover*, Marguerite Duras writes, *I often think of the image only I can see now, and of which I've never spoken.* At last setting it down for the record, against the vividness of the Mekong River:

It carries everything along, straw huts, forests, burned-out fires, dead birds, dead dogs, drowned tigers and buffaloes, drowned men, bait, islands of water hyacinths all stuck together. Everything flows towards the Pacific, no time for anything to sink, all is swept along by the deep and head- long storm of the inner current, suspended on the surface of the river's strength.

Our relationship with the past and those who populate it is constantly shifting, as is our awareness of the ways in which it has shaped us. Sometimes those things that have lain a long time, a lifetime, half-buried in silt, are washed out gleaming, as if new, returning to lay claim to us.

It's a phenomenon true to many who live to older age, regardless of lucidity or neuro- logical condition or the vocational propensity to self-mythologise. Early events shimmering up from whatever cerebral oubliette, redeclaring themselves with a vividness that is almost material, and that dulls the immediate into background. These revisitations are as authentic to life as life's mundanities.

In returning to our first stories, those most deeply etched, are we seeking the comfort of ordinance established by myth – the familiar arrangements and foretokenings a means of telling the story of ourselves so that we might reconcile ourselves to an ending?

It is likely that Farmer suspected she had Parkinson's while in residence at the Rome studio, in the autumn of 2010. She travelled the year after winning the Patrick White Award, which honours underrecognised Australian writers (necessarily late enough in a career to justify such a call). Farmer was ambivalent about accolades, and this one in particular. She told the *Age* books editor Jason Steger that she'd thought the award in effect 'an obituary' for creative life. She had wanted to contact previous recipients: 'I wanted to write to them and say please don't give up, don't let this make you feel that it's all over.'

Through 'A Ring of Gold', we are again being asked: *what lasts?*

> *As for a clean sweep, high tide, high time she put her mind to it closer to home. Out with the clutters of seashells, pebbles and river stones, nuts and leaves, feathers black and white, drops of bottle glass, the red and blue crab claws and papery carapaces, the skulls and bones she has walked blindly past, and added to, while they*

and she gathered cobwebs and dust and lost track
of where they came from and how they washed
up here. Those of the earth she takes and scatters
in the scrub of the clifftop. For those of the sea
she finds a pool in the cliff shadow with the tide
rolling in, where some settle, some shuttle down,
some float.

The ring, she has already pitched back into the sea.

But it is, after all, fiction, only one of innumerable possible endings. Taki sends me a photograph of the titular ring, posing on its watermarked envelope, found on a beach in Greece some years ago.

As for the sea clutter, the keepsakes and talismans: 'In fact, every single item in the quote – seagull skulls, feathers, shells and so forth – she was never able to return to the sea and the land … When I packed them down after her death they sat on that same cupboard all dusty and cobwebbed. I didn't know what to do with them – I couldn't part with anything too much back then, but these were also sacred in a way. They had touched her psyche and moved her somehow.'

In respite care, a place she called The Lodge, some of the nurses humoured her when she spoke of the book she had to finish. Others thought her delusional. She didn't feel the need to prove otherwise.

Once she had completed the manuscript for *This Water*, Taki tells me, 'It was as though the lifeforce went out of her.' Her eyesight had diminished to all but light and shade, but she heard the first reviews, among them Anna MacDonald for *Australian Book Review*: *She is a stylist unlike any other living Australian writer, and it is difficult to read this last work without a haunting sense of loss.*

Ivor Indyk, Farmer's editor for eighteen years, wrote in memoriam:

> *Beverley was as clear-eyed about what was coming as she was about what she sought in her writing ... I think, despite her awareness of the presence of death, she was fundamentally optimistic, a primitivist in her way, assured of the relatedness of all things, and therefore of their survival through time.*

In the Greek village she had feared would forget her, the passing bell was rung at the news of her death, and her former in-laws lit candles and mourned for one of their own.

~

Beverley Farmer asked that her ashes be scattered in a place known only to family, and was adamant that no permanent memorial be left for her. In a sense, the Bellarine Peninsula serves as well as one.

> Tides mould the beach. Sand as well as water is always in motion, now thick and smooth, now so thin and gnawed away that the bedrock stands out, gaunt, from the seawall, the dunes, down into the shallows ... The sea wears holes and rings in the limestone, caves and tunnels, wears it wholly away in time, but not smooth. On these beaches, hidden or laid bare, the rock is all as crusty and finely fretted as coral and as sharp underfoot, sandy-coloured, but not sandstone. Limestone is the bedrock of these beaches where we walk in the flesh while we may; and limestone is made of the bones and shells of the dead.

How stubborn life is, when you think, lodging its residue in the worn old skin of the earth until some convulsion crumples it into mountains, studded with coiled and spiny fossils from the earliest beginnings …

In the first version of 'A Ring of Gold', a last summer swim ends in disaster. The tide surges abruptly and the woman, the widow, is dashed against the rocks, regaining consciousness on the sand amid a crowd of onlookers who relay the damage she is not yet aware of: *just about scalped, like a skun rabbit.*

Though unable to speak, she demands silently, *why did they have to come along and interfere?*

The final version at first looks to end in much the same way. In the last hot spell, the swimmer braves the surf beach, the Mountains of the Moon, which she named as a girl for its air of remoteness, *with no other landmark seaward.*

As in the first iteration, the tide swings violently. *The current would always haul her stumbling on to hidden rocks ... pull her out of her depth.*

Yet in this second telling, there is no scene of recovery on the shore; the swimmer stays under, in a place she named in childhood.

PATTERNS OF RETURN

I'd been somewhere in the foothills of the second essay when I slid *The Bone House* back onto the shelf at the studio in Rome with that bewildering sense of impasse.

If you were to go looking for evidence of Farmer's influence in my writing, there's nothing to see. But from first opening *The Bone House*, I recognised that her words would have significant bearing on my work.

I've written here of her two hybrid works, those categorised as 'misc' or 'other' – *The Bone House* and *A Body of Water* – and 'A Ring of Gold', the opening story of her final collection, *This Water*. Farmer's seven other works of fiction are out of print.

During the course of writing this essay,

Farmer's publisher, Giramondo, announced a reissue of *A Body of Water*. Ivor Indyk has previously noted the difficulty of bringing readers to Farmer's ambitious, genre-defying works. I asked the obvious – why, then?

He speaks with admiration of the expansiveness developed through Farmer's later books – the roving style more typically viewed as a masculine ambition – and how her mastery of it helped to claim this territory for women. 'Contemporary nonfiction, particularly by women essay-writers, exhibits a similar willingness to merge formal distinctions in a more capacious mode of argument ... In relation to them, you can see Farmer as a pioneer.'

He considers the discursive an aspect of Australian provincialism that ought to be proclaimed: 'the encyclopedic tendency to find the whole world in its remotest corner'.

That was she.

Part of what I admire about Farmer is her sincerity and unabashed delight at the smallest discoveries, when earnestness has become gauche, and sensitivity has become confused with sentimentality. For all her meditative intricacies, she never gets beyond shouting distance of that bigger, biggest, frankly unseemly question of *What, exactly, are we doing here?*

She finds particles of the answer in places few would think to look.

On periwinkles: *[they] will go on for months responding in the flesh to the memory of the tidal rhythms of that original place. How can a living thing in a blue crumb of a shell no bigger than the pupil of an eye have a knowledge of the sea so vast that it outweighs absence?*

~

Earlier, I wrote that in Rome I was not yet lonely. It's true that I have a high threshold for solitude, even a dependency on it. But partway into the stay, something caught up with me. As though the drift of the past several years finally surged up and overtook me. (A plunge, a plummet. *This far and no further.*)

I longed for old friends, for family, with a new and acute urgency. Home was too elusive and perhaps still too risky a concept. But I longed for something solid, constant. Most of all, for the few people I am close enough with to be quiet alongside. Only: these few are placed so distantly apart.

For most of us, home is people as much as place. I grew up without a stable sense of either: the volatile and dangerous atmosphere in our house made me so unwell that at age five I was sent to live for a year with distant relatives in East Gippsland. If I'd stayed there, in the rhythm of regular sleep and regular meals, wading horses into the river on hot weekends, perhaps things might have been otherwise. As it is, I gave that detail – the horses – to a woman in a novel instead.

My relationship to home in adulthood, as I am coming to see it, has been to negotiate it with a kind of contingency mindset: if I stowed it with enough people, over enough ground, then it could never be wholly revoked or destroyed. And this disparate, multifaceted, mostly immaterial model does have its merits. Though it does in a sense consign one to a perpetual state of ambient longing. And it is proving, in many ways, increasingly unsustainable.

The final weeks I spent working on this book coincided with the escalation of the coronavirus from epidemic to pandemic, from global uncertainty to global crisis. Visions of empty cities were beamed around like eerie kitsch, famous landmarks and cinematic boulevards without the human scale. I scrawled early notes in mid-2019, sitting in the cavernous reading room at New York Public Library, and checked over final details in a terrarium-sized apartment in Melbourne a year later, at a time in which lending networks had become a more ad hoc, grassroots affair; books dropped by friends into letterboxes, or loaded into bicycle panniers and ferried between suburbs. Exactly twenty-four months after I first opened *The Bone House*, a friend wrote to me from lockdown in Italy: *Some reflection of the Ancient Rome reached us today. It's like hearing the thoughts from some classical artist from the past.*

We speak of this time as an intermission, a hiatus. Of course, life continues to spool out within the holding pattern. Attaining anything like equanimity demands the small feat of balancing the distant, longer prospect (some hopeful version of it) alongside deliberate attendance to the immediate. The middle distance has become precarious, freighted with so many small and large uncertainties. How many seasons will slip past before I see those who most embody home – if at a distance of several dozen latitudes? Those who, for the time being, bookend my days in interhemispheric video calls and audio messages: I wake in Melbourne to tree frogs peeping in the New York woods; lake sounds from southern Ontario; lines from W. S. Merwin's 'The Speed of Light':

it was only as the afternoon lengthened on its
dial and the shadows reached out farther and farther
*   from everything that we began to listen for what*
might be escaping us and we heard high voices ringing

I am fortunate in that what my apartment lacks in square footage, it makes up for in sky. From my desk I look out into the polychromatic awnings of trees, native and introduced: maple and magnolia, banana palm and grevillea; the street-lining standards of ailanthus and planes; the river red gums, cypress pines and Moreton Bay fig trees of the park and nearby canal. Their various branches flashing with lorikeets, rosellas, galahs, currawongs, white cockatoos, wrens, wattlebirds, honeyeaters, along with the more suburban contingent of magpies, minahs, ravens, sparrows. Occasionally the great egret who deigns to rest on the brutalist residence next door, imperiously unphased by the willy wagtail who makes darting, quixotic attempts to shoo it off.

Along with many others whose orbits have been abbreviated to this more domestic scale,

I am looking and listening more avidly to the world at hand. Attempting to match songs to their birds. Noting the particulars of foliage across the seasons, the plane trees shedding their leaves to reveal great shaggy nests (whose?). The telltale silhouettes of welcome swallows at dusk, darting through autumnal branches, though they were named by Gould as harbingers of spring. 'Our passerines are disappointingly dis-organised in their travels,' a bird-savvy friend writes. When I ask if there's a trick to looking, he tells me that 'at least half of it is listening'.

And we know this, in the abstract. We know that we hear with greater acuity for paying prolonged, intimate attention – learning to distinguish between certain noise-makers, for example – in the way we tend to notice things more frequently, more vividly, once we find, or are given, the language for them.

Farmer's work reveals how solitude can deepen our capacity for perception. It is perception as practice. In all of her writing there is a conscious effort to look long and deeply at immediate surrounds, to bring them into focus, into language – or languages – the better to recognise and comprehend. She wrote with a deep assuredness in continuity, in the metamorphic power of art to give lasting form to the transient – the *emanation of the referent*, the meaning that lives beyond the moment.

It was within another, more clearly delimited solitude that I discovered the writing of Beverley Farmer. *Discovered* in the incidental, tangible sense, which has become rarer and rarer: a book on a shelf that simply draws you to it, and you meet it free of any preconception, or obligation towards commentary. I met it, in other words, on its own terms. Appreciating that every encounter with a text is influenced by the circumstances in which we read. The conditions from which we enter, and to which we return when we lift our attention from the page, have bearing on wherever we are taken for the time in between. *A book is too small to live in, but you make yourself small enough while you're in it, and ever after, and whenever it comes to mind.* The best books – the best artworks – have a reciprocal influence on how we engage with whatever place we resurface to. As Farmer might have it, *The same note struck in two pieces of music playing in different rooms.*

WORKS BY BEVERLEY FARMER

STORIES

Milk (1983)

Home Time (1985)

Collected Stories (1987)

Place of Birth (1990)

This Water: Five Tales (2017)

NOVELS

Alone (1980)

The Seal Woman (1992)

The House in the Light (1995)

OTHER

A Body of Water: A Year's Notebook (1990)

The Bone House (2005)

MILLS & BOON

—— JOIN US ——

Sign up to our newsletter to stay up to date with...

- Exclusive member discount codes
- Competitions
- New release book information
- All the latest news on your favourite authors

Plus...
get $10 off your first order.
What's not to love?

Sign up at millsandboon.com.au/newsletter